THE POCKET

The Pocket Book of Stress Busters

Written by Kim Wilson

Edited by Ann Jaloba

Kim Wilson is a qualified Cognitive Hypnotherapist and NLP Practitioner and has been in practice since 2009. She is a regular contributor to an online magazine called *Perception* and is a co-founder of PractisePlus and SupervisionPlus whose aim is to increase the knowledge and quality of hypnotherapy support and training. Kim lives in Kent with her partner and dog.

Ann Jaloba is a qualified practising hypnotherapist, supervisor and author. Her books include *FirstDays: how to set up a therapy business and stay sane* and *The Hypnotherapy Handbook*. She is a co-founder of PractisePlus and Supervision Plus.

THE POCKET BOOK OF STRESS BUSTERS

All rights reserved. No part of this publication may be reproduced in any form (including electronically) without the written permission of the copyright owner except in accordance with the provisions of the Copyright Designs and Patents Act 1988.

Application for permission to reproduce should be directed to the publisher.

ISBN-13: 978-1511499569

ISBN-10: 1511499567

Published by Tapton New Publishing, 26 Tapton Mount Close, Sheffield S10 5DJ

copyright © Kim Wilson Ann Jaloba 2014 the moral right of the authors have been asserted

THE POCKET BOOK OF STRESS BUSTERS

DEDICATION

For anyone who thinks they can't

- you can

Introduction: understanding the nervous system

Hello and welcome to the pocket book of stress busters. Whether you are looking for a short-term fix or long-term strategies I hope you will find something useful here. I have included techniques and suggestions that are relevant for both work stress and home stress and my hope is that if you find even one of these tips helpful then this book would have done its job well.

What follows is a basic overview of the autonomic nervous system (ANS) and how it relates to our stress response. The autonomic nervous system regulates many of the body's functions without us being consciously aware of it. It regulates our breathing, blood pressure and the functions of our internal organs and is always working. It is divided into three parts, although it is the first two that we are going to be focusing on:

- The sympathetic nervous system
- The parasympathetic nervous system
- The enteric nervous system

So what happens when we are stressed? Well the whole purpose of the stress response is to allow us to effectively manage a life-threatening situation. Our system switches from prioritising our long-term survival needs to prioritising our short-term survival needs.

The sympathetic nervous system - fight or flight

When we are faced with a threat our sympathetic nervous system is stimulated. It puts us on high alert and enhances our chance of survival by enabling us to respond quickly to the situation, our blood pressure increases, our heart beats faster and our digestion slows down. These changes enable us to either react to the threat or to run away from it.

The parasympathetic system - rest and digest

When the threat has passed our parasympathetic system is stimulated producing feelings of relaxation and calm, it's why we often feel tired after a traumatic event. The parasympathetic system can now work to save energy. Our blood pressure drops, digestion can start and our pulse rate begins to slow down.

These two systems work symbiotically. Although they are both continually active when one is stimulated the other is dormant and vice versa. Unfortunately it is becoming more and more common for people to experience an almost constant arousal of the sympathetic nervous system due to excessive demands that exceed their ability to cope with them.

The causes of stress can vary from person to person, what makes one person anxious may not affect someone else. However there are some common themes, so to make things as easy as possible I have broken everything into three parts: Understanding your stress, this is where will find the most common themes or causes of stress, top tips, to help you deal with your stress and some inspirational quotes just to show you that you are not alone.

This book isn't intended as an in-depth look at stress and its effects, but as a practical aid and friend in your head reminding you that there are certain things that you can do to help take control and create a better balance in your life.

Kim Wilson, Author

THE POCKET BOOK OF STRESS BUSTERS

How to use this book

Start by turning the page and measuring your stress by taking the Stress Test and the Stress Test Scale. This will not only tell you how stressed you are at the moment, you can also take the tests again later to see how well this book is working for you.

Often stress feels overwhelming and uncontrollable so this book explains how stress works in the 'Understanding your Stress' sections. Once you understand how your body and mind are creating your stress and why, it is much easier to get in control and get the outcome you want.

There are many quick simple things you can do to help yourself every day and this is where the 'Top Tips' come in. Now you understand your stress better, you can choose the tips most helpful to you.

Finally, there are the 'Stress Busting Sayings'. Many famous and respected people have grappled with these issues and you can benefit from their insights.
Be well and happy.

Ann Jaloba, Editor

Measuring your stress: **stress test**

The following is a list of some of the common warning signs of stress. Tick any that you experience on a weekly basis.

1. Feelings of frustration or anger

2. Racing or pounding heart

3. Feelings of agitation

4. Shallow or irregular breathing

5. Feeling on edge

6. Headaches

7. Stiff neck or shoulders

8. Digestive disturbances

9. Cold or sweaty palms

10. Frequent urination

Measuring your stress: **stress test scale**

As we all have different tolerance levels to stress and areas of life that we find stressful you may find it useful to circle the number that corresponds to your experience of stress in the following areas. If you feel you have 'little or no stress' circle 1 or if you are 'extremely stressed' circle 10.

1. Work   1 2 3 4 5 6 7 8 9 10

2. Family   1 2 3 4 5 6 7 8 9 10

3. Social Life   1 2 3 4 5 6 7 8 9 10

4. Finances   1 2 3 4 5 6 7 8 9 10

5. Health   1 2 3 4 5 6 7 8 9 10

6. Living Situation 1 2 3 4 5 6 7 8 9 10

7. Neighbourhood   1 2 3 4 5 6 7 8 9 10

If you are experiencing at least two of the warning signs and have scored an 8 or higher in at least 2 of the categories then you are probably experiencing high levels of daily stress.

Understanding your stress: **too much to do**

If one of the things that causes you stress is having so much to do that it can seem overwhelming then read on. When we have too much on our plate we can't see the wood for the trees and stress builds as more and more things get added. By the end of the day we feel exhausted and have actually achieved very little.

The simplest way to begin to relieve the stress of having too many tasks is to prioritise them. Don't worry, I can already hear you shouting: "but they are all important!" Even if all the jobs you need to do are essential, I hope to give you some mental clarification regarding prioritisation that will enable you to start and finish one job at a time.

STRESS-BUSTING SAYINGS

"If you want to conquer the anxiety of life, live in the moment, live in the breath."

AMIT RAY

TOP TIP: **GLASS BALL OR RUBBER BALL**

Whether we are in full-time employment, part-time work or are full-time homeworkers, we all have things that we NEED to get done in a day. This can be as simple as walking the dog, doing the laundry or picking the kids up from school. It may be a call that has to be made or a report that has to be written; all of us have things that are important for us to complete.

The first thing to do is make a list of all the things that you need to do (lists are great when they are used well - more about that later). When you've written your list, I want you to look at each item on it and think of what would happen if you dropped that item from your things to do today. Would it bounce like a rubber ball i.e. could you do it tomorrow or would it break like a glass ball i.e. it is a project that has a hard deadline that will have adverse consequences if not done.

As you go through your list, be ruthless. Although we often think that everything has to be done right now, a lot of our tasks are rubber balls. For example, I see a lot of people who are homeworkers running a busy household. They often say that they have to do the laundry, they must do the vacuuming, and they need to pick up their children from school.

When you think about it, only of those things is a glass ball - collecting the children from school. Vacuuming and laundry are rubber balls - if you don't do them today what are the adverse consequences? I would guess that they would be very slight.

This technique is also useful for work. Your boss has asked you to do a handful of things on top of the already mountainous stack of work sitting on your desk. Make a list and go through each item, G - glass ball or R- rubber ball. Even if you find half the stack will bounce into tomorrow then you've halved your stress for that day.

This is your first level of prioritisation.

TOP TIP: **KITTEN OR LION**

So you've been through your list, you've been ruthless but no matter how many times you look at it all your items on the list have a big fat G besides them, what now?

If there is absolutely no doubt in your mind that all the things you have to do that day are glass balls and that by not doing any one of them there will be serious consequences then let me introduce you to prioritisation by consequence, otherwise known as would you rather be bitten by a kitten or a lion.

Prioritisation isn't always easy especially if we are already in a state of stress when we are trying to decide what to do first. Sometimes looking at the consequence of not doing something can give us a different perspective and help us make an informed decision.

So imagine that you have 20 things that you have to do today - they are all made of very delicate glass and you have no doubt that each would break if were not completed immediately. Look at each item on your list and think about the consequence of not doing it.

Some tasks on your list will have a bigger consequence than others. Not doing the laundry for example could be considered as having a small consequence, a bit like being bitten by a kitten. The damage will be small and superficial. You may not have a pair of clean socks for tomorrow, but that is unlikely to be life changing. Missing an important deadline at work however may have much more damaging consequences; it could mean that your ability to do your job is questioned or that you lose an important deal. It's more like being bitten by a lion, the damage is much greater and there is most certainly a longer recovery period to get back to where you were.

If you know that whatever you do you are going to receive a bite then would you rather be bitten by a kitten or a lion? Prioritise your lion tasks and then if you have time go and play with the kittens.

TOP TIP: **KISS THE FROG**

The prioritisation is going well, you're bouncing balls and wrestling lions but there's still one thing that stresses you so much you can barely look at it. It lurks in the corner growing bigger each day.

It's green and warty and in no way attractive. We've all experienced this at some time. It's the really important job that you just don't want to do.

You know that if you drop it, it will certainly break and you have no doubt that it will come and bite you on the backside at some point in the future, but you just can't face it. There is no easy way out, you need to go and Kiss that Frog.

Leaving a job that is unpleasant does nothing for our motivation. We can complete everything else on our list but our stress will not go away until we smooch with the warty one.

One of the best ways to tackle an unpleasant job is to prepare a reward for yourself after you've completed it. What we find rewarding varies from person to person so think of something that you would really look forward to doing after you've kissed your frog. It doesn't have to be something big or ambitious.

For some people a promise of a 10-minute break from work is enough to get them puckering up. The reward just has to be meaningful for you and make sure that you actually do it - our brains love rewards, they make us feel great.

The more we pair a pleasant experience with an unpleasant one the more likely we are to complete unpleasant jobs. That's how a spoonful of sugar got everyone taking their medicine.

Understanding your stress: when there is not enough time

Are you constantly worried about time? There's just not enough of it to do all those things that you need or want to do? Let's talk about the basics.

If time is your main area of stress then you need to get a realistic perspective of how much time you have versus how much time you need.

People who find time stressful tend to fall into two distinct camps.

Let's call them Camp A and Camp B.

Camp A are those people that are always surprised by how much time it takes them to do something. If you find that you are constantly late or running behind schedule then it's likely that you fall into camp A.

If you are a Camp A person, you are more likely to try to squeeze just one more thing in before you leave for that important appointment or tell your boss that you will have his project done in two hours when it's more likely to take you two days.

If on the other hand you are a Camp B person, you will find that you have trouble getting anything done because there just doesn't seem to be enough time in which to do it. Even so, you are consistently early for appointments or waiting for everyone else to get dressed when you are ready to leave the house then you are more likely to fall into Camp B.

STRESS-BUSTING SAYINGS

"Our stresses, anxieties, pains and problems arise because we do not see the world, others, or even ourselves as worthy of love."

PREM PRAKASH

TOP TIP: **HAPPY CAMPERS**

Whether you fall into camp A or B the first step is to get some perspective on time. It may sound counter-intuitive to add one more thing to your to do list every day, yet keeping a time diary is really useful.

Campers tend to be inaccurate when estimating how long it will take them to do something.

Those in Camp A tend to underestimate the time needed for tasks while those in Camp B tend to overestimate the time needed for tasks.

Let me give you an example of what may be a typical start to the day for both camps and how they may differ.

Campers in both the A and the B camps get up, shower or shave, get dressed and eat breakfast.

As Camper A tends to underestimate the time needed for any activity their estimation of how long each activity takes may read something like this.

- Get up 8am
- Shower/shave 8.15
- Get dressed 8.30
- Finish breakfast 8.45am

As Camper B tends to overestimate the time needed for any activity so their estimation of the same tasks may read something like this.

- Get up 8am
- Shower/shave 8.45
- Get dressed 9.15
- Finish breakfast 9.45am

Keeping a time diary enables both camps to build a more accurate picture of how long each activity takes and although it's a bit more work in the beginning it will reap long-term rewards.

So how do you do it? It's easy; all you need to do is to time each activity. So make a note of the time before you go for a shower and then when you've finished. Do the same before and after you get dressed. Do the same again for breakfast, I'm sure you get the picture. You only really need to do this for a couple of weeks over several different activities before you will know whether you over-estimate or underestimate the time it takes you complete tasks.

Long term this will enable you to adjust your perspective and allow you to build in or reduce time in your estimates. The amount of under or over estimation will vary from person to person so you whether you need to double the amount of time you think it will take you to do something or reduce it by a third it doesn't matter.
Try it for yourself and you can look forward to happy camping

STRESS-BUSTING SAYINGS

"Allow yourself to see what you don't allow yourself to see."

MILTON ERICKSON

TOP TIP: **ONLY ONE THING**

If you are still finding it difficult to manage your time and the amount you have to do within it then this may help. Most of our stress is caused by our own negative thinking. 'I have too much to do'; 'I'll never get it done,' and similar thoughts. Often when we are in a negative cycle of self-talk we end up doing nothing at all so the following day presents an even bigger mountain to climb.

To break the cycle, I want you to think of doing just one thing. It doesn't matter what it is or how big a task it is, just pick something. Having trouble choosing? Pick the first thing on your list or the first thing that comes to mind or the thing that you are looking forward to doing most - it's not important where you start. It's a bit like rolling a rock down a hill, all the effort goes into getting it moving in the first place once it starts rolling the momentum virtually takes over.

So if you were to do just one thing today to get that rock moving what would you choose?

STRESS-BUSTING SAYINGS

"For fast-acting relief,

try slowing down."

LILY TOMLIN

TOP TIP: **WORRY TIME**

You may have heard people talking about good stress and bad stress. What do we mean by good stress and bad stress?

Good stress really just refers to being challenged either mentally or physically, but within your capacity to cope. This can often act as a motivator. It's what makes us excited and nervous and often comes with a feeling of a sense of achievement once we've completed the challenge. Think bungee jump or public speaking.

Bad stress on the other hand is when we have been trying to manage demands that are just too much for us to cope with; this can be anything from having to look after a sick relative, to ongoing work demands, to coping with a fear of redundancy.

The stress we experience that is ongoing and not easy to manage often overtakes our thoughts. It becomes a constant mind mantra; 'must do…what if…have to …'. So this next suggestion is for anyone who can't seem to think about anything other than the things that cause them stress.

Commit to this for the following two weeks; set aside 15 minutes a day that is solely for the purpose of worrying.

You may be thinking that it seems a bit extreme or that you would rather try to focus on positive things. That's all good, but I would like you to consider how often throughout the day either you think about the thing that is causing you stress or you spend time trying to push that thought away.

Giving yourself permission to worry is a great way to focus your mind and encourage it to only spend that limited amount of time in the pursuit of that worry. Fifteen minutes may seem like a long time to worry about one particular thing, but I suspect you are already spending much longer doing it anyway. This way once your worry time is over you are free to get on with your day.

If you want to take it a step further write down everything that comes to mind in that 15 minutes whilst thinking about your issue you may be surprised how often, if you allow it to, your mind will provide you with some very interesting insights.

STRESS-BUSTING SAYINGS

"One of the symptoms of an approaching nervous breakdown is the belief that one's work is terribly important."

BERTRAND RUSSELL

Understanding your stress: **procrastination**

Procrastination is without doubt one of the most frustrating and stressful conditions that anyone can suffer.

Okay that may be a bit dramatic, but if we added up all the time that is wasted because of it I would guess that it would be a substantial number of hours. Just imagine, all the time you worry about not having enough time to do all the things you need to do and then combine that with procrastination. It makes for a day full of worry.

So here are a few ideas to get you organised and moving on with your tasks.

STRESS-BUSTING SAYINGS

"To sit with a dog on a hillside on a glorious afternoon is to be back in Eden, where doing nothing was not boring - it was peace."

MILAN KUNDERA

TOP TIP: **LISTS ARE YOUR FRIENDS**

Lists are really useful tools if they are used in the right way. They can be organised in a variety of ways, prioritised and even split into distinct categories to make them seem more doable, for example a separate list for home chores and work chores. But lists can also be an area of stress. Reams and reams of tasks that just keep being added to do not inspire a procrastinator to get going.

So I want to share two secrets about list making that will make them seem like your new bestie.

Only ever put the maximum of seven items on your list. Yes I know you have more than seven, but you will just have to make more lists. Although this may seem counter-intuitive, any more than seven items on any one list can seem overwhelming.

Try it. Write one really long list and then two or three shorter lists.

The shorter lists will look more achievable and as this particular technique is targeted at the procrastinators anything that can make things look easier is a winner. Our brains work on rewards. The more we get the more we want.

Remember when gold stars were given out at school for a job that was well done. Well, this is the equivalent. You don't actually have to go out and buy stickers but it is very important that once a task is completed that you cross it off. Each time you cross an item off your list your brain gets a small reward and you get a boost of feel-good chemicals that motivate you to do more of the same.

TOP TIP: **SMALL CHUNKS PLEASE**

Often when we put off doing a task it's because the task seems too big. We look at the whole thing and it can feel like a mammoth undertaking. However any task can be broken down into smaller chunks. I often use decorating a room as a way of explaining how small chunks work.

Imagine a room; it's full of furniture and lots of stuff. If we think about decorating that room it can seem overwhelming because there's too much to do. We have to move furniture, repair walls, take pictures down, pack up books, cover the carpets, remove the curtains etc, etc.

However if we see it as a series of small chunks or tasks it becomes much easier. So think about the first thing that you can do to make a start. This might be taking the pictures off the wall, great that's all you have to do today. Next task may be packing up the books or ornaments, just do that.

By taking the job and breaking it down into small achievable chunks it becomes much easier to imagine doing it and we are more likely to make a start. And sooner than you might imagine you will have a nice clear room just waiting to be painted. So next time something seems too big to handle just think small chunks.

STRESS-BUSTING SAYINGS

"Remain calm in every situation, because peace equals power."

JOYCE MEYER

TOP TIP: **FLICK THE SWITCH**

If procrastination is still creating an issue for you then change tasks. Sometimes all it takes to get moving again is to do something different.

This doesn't mean losing an hour on social media or watching your favourite TV show. It means changing to one of the other tasks on your list of things to do. This works most effectively if the tasks are different. If you have paperwork to do and procrastination is getting in the way then choose something new like making those calls that you've been putting off.

The same principle can be applied whatever work you do or if you are doing home tasks so have a go and flick the switch.

STRESS-BUSTING SAYINGS

"If you can change your mind you can change your life."

WILLIAM JAMES

Understanding your stress: **how to manage it in the moment**

You're in the middle of a big messy stress attack, what do you do? Sometimes all the planning, preparing and techniques will not be enough to prevent a stress attack.

Stress attacks are most likely to occur when something unexpected happens such as sleeping through your alarm clock or your boiler breaking down in the middle of winter.

The first thing you need to do to manage your stress is to breathe. Yes you are already breathing, it's unlikely that you will forget to do it, but when we are stressed we tend to breathe in a particular way.

The stress response is designed to prepare us to run away or fight whatever the immediate threat is. In order to do that we need to pump air quickly into our lungs so we can oxygenate our limbs to prepare them for movement. When we breathe in this way we tend to breathe high in our chests whereas when we are relaxed we breathe from our stomachs. So focusing on your breath is a powerful way to keep yourself calm.

STRESS-BUSTING SAYINGS

"Nothing gives a person so much advantage over another as to remain always cool and unruffled under all circumstances."

THOMAS JEFFERSON

TOP TIP: 7/11 **BREATHING**

Start by just noticing your breath. Is it short and ragged? Do you notice your chest rising and falling more than your stomach? Do you feel out of breath or that your breath is restricted?

As you breathe begin to count, although this breathing technique is often referred to as 7/11 breathing it's important to count to whatever number you feel comfortable with.

If your immediate in-breath is short and you can only manage a steady count of 5 then that is fine. The point of the exercise is that as you breathe out you will be extending that breath. Breathing out for a count of 11 to encourage a full out-breath that extends down into your stomach. Breathing in for a count of 7 and out for a count of 11. It's important that the out-breath last longer than the in-breath because the out-breath stimulates the body's natural relaxation response. By changing your pattern of breathing in this way, your body automatically begins to relax.

Do this for 10 to 20 breaths concentrating on the counting. If your mind wanders gently bring it back. If paying attention to your breath makes you more anxious stop and try again another day. If counting causes you an issue then try the next suggestion.

STRESS-BUSTING SAYINGS

"Your work is going to fill a large part of your life, and the only way to be truly satisfied is to do what you believe is great work, and the only way to do great work is to love what you do. If you haven't found it yet keep looking. Don't settle, as with all matters of the heart, you'll know when you find it."

STEVE JOBS

TOP TIP: BREATHING CALM AND RELAXED

This is a variation of 7/11 breathing. Counting creates an issue for some people - not that they can't count but many people find it irritating so this is just an alternative.

Although I have suggested the words calm and relaxed you can use anything that is meaningful to you, just make sure that your out-breath-word is longer than your in-breath-word.

The principle is exactly the same, as you breathe in say the word 'calm' in your head and as you breathe out say the word 'relaxed'. If your mind wanders gently bring it back to focus on the words.

TOP TIP: **FISTS AND FEET**

Although it may sound counter-intuitive to bring more tension to your body when it is stressed it can work wonders. There may be times when you can't action the feet part of this technique but that's fine try it with just the fists and see how you get on. You can also extend this technique to include your face and the rest of your body although I would suggest you do that in private. It's a really effective technique if you feel stressed before going to bed as it triggers a relaxation response in the muscles.

When you are feeling stressed, clench your fists and toes into tight balls. Really put as much effort as is comfortable, be careful if you have long fingernails as you may have to adjust how you clench your hands. Hold for a few seconds and then release.

Releasing the tension triggers a relaxation response in your muscles, focus on how your hands and feet are feeling notice the sensation of relaxation as it spreads through your fingers and toes. Repeat twice more noticing how that relaxation grows each time. If you are doing the exercise with your whole body you can either bring tension to the whole body before releasing it or work through muscle group and release them as you go, for example bring tension into your shoulders then release, followed by your upper back, then release.

STRESS-BUSTING SAYINGS

"A crust eaten in peace is better than a banquet partaken in anxiety."

AESOP

TOP TIP: **PERIPHERAL VISION**

When we experience stress we are very focused on the immediate, we have tunnel vision and can't think or see anything else. So my next suggestion is to try peripheral vision.

Choose a place to focus on that is ideally straight ahead and slightly above eye level. Keep your eyes softly focused on that spot while you begin to take your awareness to the edges of your field of vision.

Notice what you can see from the corners of your eyes not forgetting what you can see above and below your normal line of sight. Keep your eyes still and just allow your field of vision to expand. Do this for a minute or so and you may begin to notice how your body begins to relax and your breathing begins to slow down.

TOP TIP: **TAKE TEN**

Although some people experience stress wherever they are some people experience greater stress when they are in a particular territory.

Many people are stressed at work for example, but feel more relaxed at home. It's useful to know where you 'do' your stress more often because sometimes taking even a ten-minute break can relieve the stress cycle. Are you thinking that you don't have enough time to take a ten-minute break? I challenge you to think again.

If you are overly-stressed you will most likely be unproductive, short-tempered, frustrated and even too tired to do what you are meant to be doing.

A change of environment can often be the simplest way to break your stress. Unfortunately, this doesn't mean going outside for a smoke or down the pub for a quick one before coming back to tackle whatever it is that made you stressed in the first place.

The most effective stress busting environments are in nature. This doesn't necessarily mean you have to take a quick hike in the woods, but think about a walk round the block to get some fresh air and a change of scenery. If you are a homeworker then your home environment can become stressful so this advice goes out to you too.

If you think that you can take a ten-minute break in the garden instead of going out then ask yourself: are you thinking about all the things that need to be done in the garden while you are out there trying to relax? If you are, find a different environment. Allowing yourself to have a ten-minute break from stress will revitalise you and in turn make you more productive.

STRESS-BUSTING SAYINGS

"The field of consciousness is tiny. It accepts only one problem at a time."

ANTOINE DE SAINT-EXUPÉRY

THE POCKET BOOK OF STRESS BUSTERS

STRESS-BUSTING SAYINGS

"The greatest weapon against stress is our ability to chose one thought over another."

WILLIAM JAMES

Understanding your stress: **the importance of perspective**

Stress can cause us to lose perspective. We focus entirely on the issues which are stressing us and forget that in the wider scheme of things some of the stuff that we are finding stressful isn't really that important. So I have included a couple of ideas that may help you regain that perspective and find a balance.

TOP TIP: **30, 60, 90**

Time has a wonderful way of giving us perspective. Remember that really embarrassing thing you did when you were young? It probably doesn't feel anywhere near as embarrassing now as it did at the time. So I would like you to consider the following. Will the thing that you are currently stressing about be of any importance in 30, 60 or 90 days time?

That thing you absolutely have to do right now, will it have an impact on your life, will you even remember what it was in a year or two?

Stress causes us to be very short-sighted and narrowly focused. By widening our view we can often gain a better picture of what is important and what is not. Take a breath and imagine yourself in a month's time, looking back. Then in two month's time looking back. You get the picture. You can even take it to the extreme, if you are sitting in your rocking chair at the end of your very long and fulfilling life does the thing that is currently causing you to be stressed matter?

STRESS-BUSTING SAYINGS

"There is more to life the increasing its speed."

MOHANDAS K. GANDHI

TOP TIP: **WHAT'S IN YOUR BOAT?**

Imagine you are in a small rowing boat.

This is your boat and it has all your things in it. It has everything you need to be happy in life. However, as with anything that we like to call home it needs maintenance from time to time.

As you make your way down the river, sometimes rowing and sometimes drifting you pass many other boats all travelling downstream with their own people and each with their own stuff within.

Every so often you may come across someone who hasn't been looking after their boat very well and you stop to help them bail out water or to re-organise their stuff so that their boat remains afloat.

However if you do that too often and continually look into other people's boats you may find that you are neglecting the leak in your own and you begin to sink. The river suddenly seems very empty and no one is there to help you as they still have their own boats to look after. You and your boat are important, you have to come first.

This isn't encouraging you to be dispassionate about the fate of other people or to become horribly selfish.

What I want to encourage you to do is think about what's in your boat first. If your boat is in good order and someone else asks for help then great, but stop looking into other people's boats?

If you are taking on too much, trying to help too many people then your boat will sink and you will be no help to anyone in the future. So your priority should be to make sure that you are water tight and shipshape. Happy boating.

STRESS-BUSTING SAYINGS

"If a problem is fixable, if a situation is such that you can do something about it, then there is no need to worry. If it is not fixable, then there is no help in worrying. There is no benefit in worrying whatsoever."

DALAI LAMA

TOP TIP: **LIGHTEN YOUR EXPECTATIONS**

Stress can be triggered because of our own expectations of what should happen, what someone should do. This is probably one of the hardest areas to manage because accepting that other people do not think in the same way as us is actually quite difficult to understand.

I have borrowed a quote from Bruce Lee who summed it up nicely: "I'm not in this world to live up to your expectations and you're not in this world to live up to mine."

If you find that you are often disappointed by people or find yourself in situations where you think that you have to do everything yourself because no one else does it right then it could be your expectations causing the issue.

Certain personality types are prone to this type of stress. You know who you are.

You like things done your way because it's the right way and you wonder how anyone could think of doing it differently. Well it may not be what you want to hear, but I want you to consider the possibility that it wasn't the other person being difficult or useless.

In fact, they are more than capable of doing whatever it was they were meant to be doing. They just weren't doing it your way. If you understand your strengths and weaknesses and your tendency to think in a certain way then you will be in a much better position to let unnecessary expectations go. We all think differently there is no right or wrong way so give yourself and other people a break, take a step back and get some perspective.

STRESS-BUSTING SAYINGS

"Never let the future disturb you, you will meet it, if you have to, with the same weapons of reason which today arm you against the present. "

MARCUS AURELIUS

Understanding your stress: **long term planning**

Where do we go from here? You've tried the techniques and hopefully have found at least one that has proved useful to you, but how do you manage stress long term?

This next section is aimed at helping you think and feel differently about stress and gives you techniques that can use now that will enable you to manage stress in the future.

STRESS-BUSTING SAYINGS

"Do not anticipate trouble, or worry about what may never happen, keep in the sunlight."

BENJAMIN FRANKLIN

TOP TIP: JUST SAY "NO"

Go on I dare you. Does it make you feel uncomfortable? For some of us saying no is a big challenge. We don't want to seem rude or offend the other person. We want to help others and avoid conflict and sometimes we say yes to things because we are afraid of missing out on opportunities.

However saying no is one of the most important things you can do for yourself. Taking on too much is self-inflicted stress, why would you do that? So if saying no is something that you find difficult here are my top five qualifiers that may make you feel a little more at ease with it.

- I have other priorities right now I just can't commit to it.
- I'm in the middle of something. Can we discuss it at xxxx time?
- I'm not the best person to help you with this.
- No, I can't.
- I'd love to, but I just don't have the time at the moment. Can we revisit it in xxxx?

Try it, if you are in the habit of saying yes to everything and that is causing you to become stressed then practise the art of saying no, it's not as hard as it seems.

TOP TIP: **PRACTISE GRATITUDE**

It can be difficult when you are experiencing stress to be aware of anything else. Our focus is so much on what we have to do and how we feel that we forget that there are still things to be grateful for or that are going well.

So the aim of this exercise is to make a note of three things that you are grateful for each day. Write them in a journal and continue keeping this journal for a month. They don't have to be big things, it's about what's meaningful for you, it can be something as simple as your favourite song on the radio or the lack of a traffic jam on the way to work.

Purposely re-directing our thoughts toward positive events can increase our overall happiness. This reduces stress, so why not give it a try? You may like it so much that it just becomes a habit that you want to continue.

STRESS-BUSTING SAYINGS

"I am an old man and have known a great many troubles, but most of them have never happened."

MARK TWAIN

TOP TIP: SMILE - BE HAPPY

You've probably heard the old saying: "Fake it until you make it." Well, it turns out to be true. The body can't tell the difference between what's real and what's not. If you find this hard to believe, then think about how you feel when you wake up from a nightmare or watch a scary film.

There's a wonderful bit of research which demonstrates how this works. Volunteers were asked to play a simple sequence of piano notes each day for five consecutive days. Their brains were scanned each day in the region connected to the finger muscles. Another set of volunteers were asked to just imagine playing the notes instead, and they had their brains scanned each day too.

At the end of the research the scans of both groups were compared and found to be the same. So even if you don't feel like it smile. Sooner than you may think you will start to feel less stressed and more relaxed.

STRESS-BUSTING SAYINGS

"Worry is a misuse

of imagination."

DAN ZADRA

TOP TIP: **ANCHORS AWAY**

An anchor is a very effective way of changing the way you feel. If you've ever heard of the Russian scientist Ivan Pavlov and his famous dogs you will already know where this is going.

Pavlov rang a bell every time he fed his dogs and discovered that with repetition just the ringing of the bell would be enough for his dogs to begin to salivate. They had been conditioned to associate the bell with the arrival of food. Well we can do the same with a useful feeling such as calm. Have a read through the instructions before you start and feel free to use your own feelings/words in place of what I've chosen here.

1. Remember a time when you felt really calm, relaxed and in control. This is an important step so don't rush. Think about what you saw, heard and felt at that time. Make the memory as vivid as you can.

How strong is that memory ? If you were to make that memory as strong as it could be what would you need to do to that memory to make those positive feelings even more powerful?

When that memory is as strong as you feel you can get it and you are feeling those feelings of calm, relaxed and in control, squeeze the thumb and middle finger of your right hand together. By doing this you are creating an association between the pressure of your thumb and middle finger and the good feelings you are remembering.

2.   Do this at least five more times, each time create those positive feelings as fully as possible before squeezing your thumb and middle finger together. You will know when you've done enough when all you need to do is to squeeze your fingers together and you experience those feelings of calm, relaxation and control.

It's important that you don't scrimp on the above steps, we want to anchor those positive feelings to the action of squeezing your fingers together so we are aiming for a really strong association.

3.   Think of a situation in the past that you found mildly stressful. Squeeze your fingers together and feel that calm, relaxation and control spreading through your Imagine yourself handling that situation perfectly. Do you feel more relaxed and in control?

Keep practising until you can recall the feelings with ease and then try it on a current stressful situation.

STRESS-BUSTING SAYINGS

"That the birds of worry and care fly over your head, this you cannot change, but that they build nests in your head, this you can prevent."

CHINESE PROVERB

Understanding your stress: **relaxation**

Relaxation isn't something that you fit it if you have time. It is an absolute priority. Remember at the beginning of the book, I talked about our parasympathetic system being stimulated once a threat had passed? Well if it never gets activated because you are constantly under a perceived threat (too much pressure) you will remain stressed, which isn't good news for your long-term health.

Often we think we are relaxing when we are not. Examples include: watching TV, playing computer games, and having a drink after work.

All these are actually stimulants. Remember that your body and mind don't know the difference between what is real and what is imagined. Don't believe me? Then think about how you feel when you are watching something on TV that is distressing. Relaxation is about enabling both your body and mind to switch off. To allow the muscles to completely rest and to get some much needed head space.

STRESS-BUSTING SAYINGS

"As a rule, what is out of sight disturbs men's minds more seriously than what they see."

JULIUS CAESAR

TOP TIP: **BOOK TIME IN YOUR DIARY**

This may seem a little extreme, but if you don't set aside time to relax it's unlikely that you will find the time to do it.

Remember that relaxation should be a priority. This is your long-term health and happiness that we are talking about so what's more important? Even if you book 10 minutes into your busy day for meditation, 7/11 breathing or relaxation in some other way then you will really notice a difference.

STRESS-BUSTING SAYINGS

"Blessed is the person who is too busy to worry in the daytime and too sleepy to worry at night."

ANON

TOP TIP: **I AM RELAXED**

Many years ago I used to teach Yoga and this is one of the exercises that I would do at the end of the class, it often generated snores so I am including it here to help you get started. You can do it sitting or standing but preferably lying down on your back with your arms slightly away from your sides, legs relaxed. Place your awareness in the area you want to relax and repeat mentally two or three times.

I relax my feet. My feet are relaxed.

I relax my ankles. My ankles are relaxed.

I relax my calves. My calves are relaxed.

I relax my knees. My knees are relaxed.

I relax my thighs. My thighs are relaxed.

I relax my pelvis. My pelvis is relaxed.

I relax my stomach. My stomach is relaxed.

I relax my chest. My chest is relaxed.

I relax my back. My back is relaxed.

I relax my shoulders. My shoulders are relaxed.

I relax my hands. My hands are relaxed.

I relax my neck. My neck is relaxed.

I relax my face. My face is relaxed.

I relax my scalp. My scalp is relaxed.

I relax my mind. My mind is relaxed.

I am relaxed.

STRESS-BUSTING SAYINGS

"People become attached to their burdens sometimes more than the burdens are attached to them."

GEORGE BERNARD SHAW

TOP TIP: LAUGH

What makes you smile or better yet what makes you laugh out loud? Did you know that laughter therapy has a rich history and has been and is still is used to help treat cancer, AIDS and depression.

Laughter unleashes a rush of stress-busting endorphins so think about what gets you giggling. Remember that the body doesn't know the difference between what's real and what's not so if you are finding it hard to find anything funny here are some ideas to get you going. Please do try these in public, think about how good you will make other people feel as they laugh along with you. Nice and loud now.

Donkey Laugh. Imagine you are laughing in the style of a donkey, ee-haw ee-haw.

Hearty Laugh. Raise your arms above your head tilt your chin up and imagine that you are laughing from your heart.

Scary Laugh. Imagine watching a scary film, what would your laugh be like? Nervous, high-pitched? Give it a go.

Old and Young. Imagine what your laugh would sound like in ten years or 20 years. How did it sound when you were two or three?

Beethoven's Fifth. Ha ha ha haaaaaaaa, ha ha ha haaaa

I finish on this one because I love the thought of people out and about breaking out their experimental laughs.

Thank you for taking the time to read and I wish you a stress free and relaxed future.

STRESS-BUSTING SAYINGS

"Our fatigue is often caused not by work, but by worry, frustration and resentment."

DALE CARNEGIE

THE POCKET BOOK OF STRESS BUSTERS

Useful organisations and websites

www.isma.org.uk

The International Stress Management Association promotes knowledge and best practice in the prevention and reduction of human stress.

www.stress.org.uk

The Stress Management Society is a not-for profit organisation dedicated to helping people tackle stress.

www.stress.org

The American Institute of Stress (AIS) is a non-profit organisation which imparts information on stress reduction, stress in the workplace, effects of stress and other stress-related topics.

The Pocket Book of Stress Busters

Our services

If you would like one-to-one help with managing your stress contact

Kim Wilson at Sunray Hypnotherapy
www.sunrayhypnotherapy.com
or
Ann Jaloba at Wellthought Hypnotherapy
www.wellthought.co.uk

If you would like some formal training in managing stress then contact our training company PractisePlus
www.practiseplus.org

If you are a practising therapist dealing in these areas we offer a clinical practise supervision service at SupervisionPlus
www.supervisionplus.org

THE POCKET BOOK OF STRESS BUSTERS

The Pocket Book of Stress Busters

Printed in Great Britain
by Amazon.co.uk, Ltd.,
Marston Gate.